# Introducing Children to Silence and Prayer

# Introducing Children to Silence and Prayer

## For Catechists and Parents

*Luis M. Benavides*

One Liguori Drive
Liguori MO 63057-9999

Imprimi Potest:
Harry Grile, CSsR, Provincial
Denver Province, The Redemptorists

Published by Liguori Publications
Liguori, Missouri 63057

To order, call 800-325-9521
www.liguori.org

Copyright © 2013 Luis M. Benavides

All rights reserved. No part of this publication may be reproduced, stored in a retrieval system, or transmitted in any form or by any means—electronic, mechanical, photocopy, recording, or any other—except for brief quotations in printed reviews, without the prior written permission of Liguori Publications.

**Cataloging-in-Publication Data on file with Library of Congress.**

p ISBN: 978-0-7648-2314-5
e ISBN: 978-0-7648-2315-2

Excerpts from English translation of the *Catechism of the Catholic Church* for the United States of America © 1994, United States Catholic Conference, Inc.—Libreria Editrice Vaticana; English translation of the *Catechism of the Catholic Church: Modifications from the Editio Typica* © 1997, United States Catholic Conference, Inc.—Libreria Editrice Vaticana.

Excerpts from Vatican Documents used with permission. © Libreria Editrice Vaticana.

Scripture texts in this work are taken from the *New American Bible,* revised edition © 2010, 1991, 1986, 1970 Confraternity of Christian Doctrine, Washington, D.C., and are used by permission of the copyright owner. All Rights Reserved. No part of the *New American Bible* may be reproduced in any form without permission in writing from the copyright owner.

Liguori Publications, a nonprofit corporation, is an apostolate of The Redemptorists. To learn more about The Redemptorists, visit Redemptorists.com.

Printed in the United States of America
17 16 15 14 13 / 5 4 3 2 1
First Edition

*For my grandfather,
who understood silence well.*

# TABLE OF CONTENTS

Foreword ................................................... 9
Preface .................................................... 11
Introduction ............................................... 13
   The Way of Prayer ...................................... 13
   Children's Relationship with God ....................... 14

## Chapter 1
The Different Forms of Prayer ............................. 17
   Personal or Silent Prayer .............................. 18
   Community Prayer ....................................... 19
   Prayer from Memory or Memory in Prayers? ............... 23
   Psalms and Children .................................... 27
   The Lord's Prayer: Jesus' Favorite Prayer .............. 32
   Praying the Rosary ..................................... 33

## Chapter 2
Praying with the Senses ................................... 39
   Praying with the Eyes: Knowing How to LOOK ............. 40
   Praying with the Ears: Knowing How to LISTEN ........... 41
   Praying with the Hands: Knowing How to TOUCH ........... 41
   Praying with the Mouth: Knowing How to TASTE and SPEAK . 42
   Praying with the Nose: Knowing How to SMELL ............ 43

## Chapter 3
Praying Through Gestures, Singing, and Drawing ............ 45
   Gestures ............................................... 46
   Singing ................................................ 50
   Drawing ................................................ 52

## Chapter 4
Introduction to Silence .................................... 55
   The World Without Silence ............................. 55
   Silence and the Mystery of God ......................... 56
   Biblical Silence ........................................ 56
   Types of Silence ....................................... 59

## Chapter 5
Introducing Children to Silence .......................... 61
   Practical Considerations ............................... 62
   Helpful Techniques ??? ................................ 64

## Chapter 6
A Place for Prayer ........................................ 71
   The Prayer Corner ..................................... 72
   Characteristics of the "Prayer Corner" ................... 73

## Chapter 7
Prayer in the Family ...................................... 77
   From Conception to the Baby's Arrival Home ............. 78
   Before the Child Can Walk ............................. 79
   After the Child Can Walk .............................. 81
   Different Occasions to Pray ............................ 82

Conclusion ............................................... 87
Bibliography ............................................. 89

# Foreword

*"Only the spirit that is in man knows what is in man,"* the Word of God tells us. And that is truly the case, even though it has not yet been fully awakened in that little being.

For this reason, a mother looks into her baby's eyes and with gestures, tenderness, and words gradually awakens in him or her all the things of which the human spirit is capable. Among those things is language, which will allow the child to communicate with others, express feelings, and understand what he or she says. And then one day the magic word—Mommy!— comes from the child's lips. It is the same word the child's mother has repeated to him thousands of times. The word illuminates her heart and sounds like the most original declaration she has ever heard, for she feels that in this one word, the child has managed to unite himself with the one who is speaking to him. It is a sign that language has finally awakened in him.

So it is with prayer. In baptism, God gave us the Spirit of Jesus, who prays in us. At first we speak to God with incoherent babbles, until one day we manage to turn it into the language and prayer that we and others can understand, which makes our mother, the Church, happy.

Luis is an old friend of mine, though he is much younger. He is an expert in youth ministry and also in catechesis. From his rich experience with children, he leaves us a handful of suggestions, and each one will have to be sown where the winds of God make it land.

Therefore, I am glad to join these pages to bless all who work in religious education and in the catechesis of our children, especially the families and catechists who are training young Christians to enter into conscious dialogue with the Spirit they received in baptism.

+ Mamerto Menapace, OSB
Monastery of Santa María de los Ángeles
Los Toldos—Argentina

# Preface

Years ago, when I started working in children's catechesis, one of the first concerns or difficulties I encountered was the lack of methods and systematization of experiences regarding prayer with children. Basically, I was looking for ways to start teaching children how to pray. Also, many parents, teachers, and catechists were asking me how to introduce children to prayer.

After being in contact with the little ones for just a short while, I realized the issue was not as difficult as it seemed. Children have a great capacity for contemplation and admiration of the absolute, of prayer and communion with God that is less common in the adult world.

So I started to collect and exchange experiences with other catechists and parents and to seek information. However, what helped me most was to pray and to learn to pray together with the children. They became real "masters of prayer," perhaps because Jesus said, "Let the children come to me, and do not prevent them; for the kingdom of heaven belongs to such as these" (Matthew 19:13–15).

After starting with relatively scant knowledge of the subject, I gradually realized that children are able to have authentic experiences of prayer—many more spontaneous and heartfelt than those of adults who, paradoxically, often offer greater resistance to prayer.

This book is a systematic collection of various prayer experiences I've shared with children, parents, and other catechists. It is aimed at all those who feel the desire to awaken the sense of prayer in children: parents, grandparents, and other relatives; teachers and catechists; and all adults who feel the need to grow in the experience of God, hand-in-hand with the children.

One last clarification. Almost without my realizing it, this book sold out its third edition in Argentina. In addressing the work of the fourth edition, I made some revisions and additions, adding elements I've been incorporating over the years. I also found it appropriate to add some short texts of Church documents that provide helpful guidance on prayer with children. In addition, although some issues were already addressed in a previous book I wrote about children's catechetical methodology, I wanted to include them here in an expanded format as well.

My hope is that these reflections help us to better communicate with God and lead our children to pray more often and more naturally so that they make prayer a lifestyle.

**Luis M. Benavides**
lmbenavides@arnet.com.ar
or
lmbenavides@gmail.com
www.luis-benavides.go.to

# Introduction

## The Way of Prayer

Prayer is perhaps the ultimate expression of love between the creature and his Creator. Baptism establishes a relationship of love between God and child, creating in the child the power and the need to respond to that love. Encouraging the child's spiritual growth, therefore, means helping him enter freely into the reciprocity of this love relationship.

Our task consists in steering children toward an authentic life of prayer. This is not to cram the children's heads with ideas about God and train them to recite prayers by heart. Fundamentally, our goal is to teach them to live constantly in the presence of God, to live with God.

This initiation into prayer does not consist so much in talking *about* God but in talking *with* God. We need to realize that the catechetical process must become a true school of prayer. Thus we will rediscover prayer in our own lives and in catechesis.

There are no written or preset formulas for initiating people into prayer. We learn to pray by praying. It is quite evident that the light of our personal example will be the best initiation into prayer for children. The taste for prayer is contagious. It is passed on by praying and showing others the happiness that comes from living in the presence of God. Prayer is the life of the new heart, and it should encourage us at all times. However, we often forget the One who is our

Life and our All. Prayer is like a "remembrance of God," a frequent awakening of the "memory of the heart."

Children should make prayer to God the Father a lifestyle. Any time, act, or occasion can be a good reason for praise and prayer. Early on, children must internalize the presence of God as something definitive in their life. Prayer is one of the best occasions for us to live out our relationship with God spontaneously.

The child must experience a God who cares for him, loves him, and always protects him. The conviction that God is constantly with us, even in difficulties, is one of the most necessary truths in our journey through this world.

In prayer, it is the living God who reaches out to his children, and it is God who always has the last word. Prayer is a gift, so we must ask God to teach us to pray.

> *"If you knew the gift of God!" (John 4:10). The wonder of prayer is revealed beside the well where we come seeking water: there, Christ comes to meet every human being. It is he who first seeks us and asks us for a drink. Jesus thirsts; his asking arises from the depths of God's desire for us. Whether we realize it or not, prayer is the encounter of God's thirst with ours. God thirsts that we may thirst for him.*
>
> Catechism of the Catholic Church, 2560

## Children's relationship with God

*You made us for yourself, O Lord,*
*and our hearts will not rest until they rest in you.*

(*Translated from the Spanish*) Attributed to Saint Augustine

The child will grow in faith with three certainties she has learned and experienced since childhood: *God's greatness, God's love, and the human being's need for the absolute.*

The child will internalize this gradual and progressive awareness of her relationship with God as she has deep experiences of encountering God as her Father.

The child's religiosity must respond to these three fundamental aspects, which are related to the idea of God that the child is forming and which are vital needs both for her baptized soul and for her psychology.

### *God's greatness: God is their Creator*

The first trait children have to discover and experience through prayer is the *greatness of God.* God reveals himself as great, almighty, the creator of all that exists, the source of all power, strong (God always triumphs), and omnipresent (God is everywhere). God is Lord of the cosmos and of history, the unique and different one (the Holy), the transcendent one. God is the greatest of all and calls us personally to be small before him, to thank him with childlike gratitude for our creation, to worship him.

### *God's love: God is their Father*

The greatness of God is inextricably linked to his goodness. Goodness and greatness, love and omnipotence, are not contradictory terms but ideas that reinforce and complement each other.

The child's need for love will be filled by a God who loves her, takes care of her, maintains her in life, and protects and accompanies her forever.

Thus, we will speak of a God who is Love, a close and provident God, a good God who loves each and every one of us. God invites us to give thanks, to trust him, and to talk with him always. For this reason, it is necessary to discover and associate with God all that is a source of joy, beauty, light, and happiness for the child.

## *The need for the absolute: God is "their" God*

The need for a sense of wonder and the absolute arises from the child's desire for greatness, his *supernatural need for God, his desire for transcendence.*

God then appears as the completion of the creature, as the being who meets the ultimate needs of humanity's nature and the life of grace. Thus God will not be seen as something impersonal or abstract. *God will be her God, who created her, chose her, and loves her personally.*

The child will admire and contemplate his creator, his friend, his *all;* he will pay the tribute of love and respect with his life, and *prayer will be a dialogue of love between God and human beings,* between those who love each other.

Becoming aware of our relationship with God stirs up the need to pray. If we do not awaken in children a desire to pray, our catechesis will lose meaning.

*If catechesis is not up to true prayer, it is not an authentic catechesis.* Again, catechesis should not talk so much *about* God, but lead children to speak *with* God.

# Chapter 1
# The Different Forms of Prayer

*Where does prayer come from? Whether prayer is expressed in words or gestures, it is the whole man who prays. But in naming the source of prayer, Scripture speaks sometimes of the soul or the spirit, but most often of the heart (more than a thousand times). According to Scripture, it is the heart that prays. If our heart is far from God, the words of prayer are in vain.*

Catechism of the Catholic Church, 2562

*Do not be afflicted if you do not immediately receive from God what you ask of him: He wants to give you an even greater good through your perseverance with him in prayer. He wants our desire to be tested in prayer. In this way, he prepares us to receive what he is ready to give us.*

(*Translated from the Spanish*) Attributed to Saint Augustine

Every Christian, or rather, anyone who sincerely wants to communicate with his or her Lord, tries different forms of prayer throughout life. We could summarize or group them around three elements: time reserved for *personal prayer*; an *attitude of faith* that informs and inspires one's daily acts; and the *communal* celebration of that faith.

From a young age, children should be able to try out the different forms of prayer that have emerged throughout the history of God's people. Children will learn and live a form of prayer suited to each moment. Thus they will know how to praise God for everything good and beautiful that he has given us; the prayer of supplication, thanksgiving; prayer through song, gesture, and drawing; repetitive prayers; short texts from the Word of God; personal prayer; and so on.

Although there are different ways of praying, we could speak of two basic forms: personal (or silent) prayer and communal prayer. That is, individual prayer that every human being directs to his or her God and the prayer to the Father that brothers and sisters share.

## Personal or silent prayer

Children have to slowly get used to achieving spaces of inner silence. That is, they need to achieve moments of deep communication with God our Father. Personal or silent prayer is perhaps, as stated above, the ultimate expression of love between the creature and his Creator. Adoration is the first attitude of the human who recognizes that he or she is a creature before his or her Creator.

Without spaces for personal, silent prayer, there is simply no prayer or authentic catechesis. Even Jesus needed to take time to be alone with his Father. The same thing happens to every Christian: We should adopt a prayerful, open, and accepting attitude toward the greatness of God. In this field, as we will see below, being introduced to silence plays an essential role.

Children—and adults—must be able to come before God to present their concerns, fears, hopes, requests, praise, and thanks. They must grasp at all times that God is their Father and that he never leaves them, even in difficult times. Children must learn to call on God, who loves us and keeps us; on Jesus, the Son of God and our brother, who leads us to the Father; on the Holy Spirit, who dwells within us; and on Mary, the Mother of Jesus and our mother.

*It is in personal and community prayer that the disciple, fed by the Word and the Eucharist, cultivates a relationship of deep friendship with Jesus Christ and seeks to embrace the will of the Father. Daily prayer is a sign of the primacy of grace in the missionary disciple's journey. Hence, "we have to learn to pray, as it were, learning this art ever anew from the lips of the Divine Master."*

Aparecida, 255

## Community prayer

Children need to have their first experiences of community prayer at an early age. They should be able to grasp that the community—family, friends, and others—is there to pray with them, to share their joys and sorrows, to pray with them for a personal intention. A child asking her friends to pray for her sick kitty is generating a saving act of God's love.

Thus, communal expressions of the faith arise in such times of prayer with others. These moments of interpersonal encounter strengthen the certainty that others are standing alongside us, that they share the same faith. Through community prayer, children will learn:

- **The prayer of praise** for all the lovely and beautiful things God is constantly giving us through all of creation. Praise is the form of prayer that recognizes in the most direct way that God is God. Praise sings to God for his own sake, giving glory to him for who he is, not just for what he does. Praise integrates the other forms of prayer and carries them toward him who is its source and goal. The vital synthesis of praise in the Old

Testament is the Hebrew expression *"Hallelu-Ya!" (Hallelujah), "Praise the Lord!"*

- **The prayer of supplication and petition,** which not only presents all of our needs, anxieties, and fears to God, but puts us in solidarity with the rest of humankind by making us aware and responsible for all those who are in our prayers, opening us to all the personal and social problems that are out there. Praying for others, as an expression of the "communion of saints," even for our enemies, brings us to the prayer of Jesus.

- **The prayer of thanksgiving** expresses our continuing gratitude for all that God gives us and does for us each day and at every moment. We thank God because his love is infinite. "In all circumstances give thanks, for this is the will of God for you in Christ Jesus" (1 Thessalonians 5:18).

It is very important for children to pray aloud and express their own concerns, their own intentions. Children enjoy these spontaneous prayers of petition, praise, and thanksgiving, and I'm sure God does too. For as children learn to pray in this way, they also grow in their sense of communal prayer.

In that regard, we have to help children listen carefully to others' prayers so as to understand their intention or meaning. This does not mean that all prayers are to be imitated exactly or repeated by rote. We have to help children personalize their prayers as much as possible. The idea is to put a real, personal face on all prayers and always say them in the first person (singular or plural). For example:

- It's one thing to say, "I pray to the Lord for poor children…" (impersonal) and quite another to pray, "Jesus, please help those three guys I saw cleaning car windows this morning."

- It's one thing to pray "for the sick" and quite another to share with others, "Dear Jesus, I pray for my grandmother Clara, who is sick."

- It is one thing to pray "for us to be better and better" and another to pray for "so-and-so, whom I don't get along with very well, so that I can understand him better and approach him."

Through experiences of prayer with others (especially in the celebration of the Word), children gradually become aware of the great communal prayer of the Church, the liturgy, which reaches its maximum expression in the Mass, or Eucharist. Unfortunately, we tend to move away from communal prayer as we grow older, move away from sharing our lives.

> *Catechesis cannot be limited to merely doctrinal formation, but it must be a true school of integral formation. Hence, friendship with Christ in prayer, appreciation for liturgical celebration, shared experience in community, and apostolic commitment through ongoing service to others must be cultivated.…Hence, it will become imperative that there be warm spaces of community prayer to feed the fire of an irrepressible zeal and make possible an attractive testimony of unity so "that the world may believe" (John 17:21).*
>
> Aparecida, 299 and 362

The *Catechism of the Catholic Church* (2626–2638) describes the Church's forms of prayer, as follows:

### I. Blessing and Adoration

Blessing *expresses the basic movement of Christian prayer: it is an encounter between God and man. In blessing, God's gift and man's acceptance of it are united in dialogue with each other. The prayer of blessing is man's response to God's gifts: because God blesses, the human heart can in return bless the One who is the source of every blessing.*

Adoration *is the first attitude of man acknowledging that he is a creature before his Creator. It exalts the greatness of the Lord who made us and the almighty power of the Savior who sets us free from evil.*

## *II. Prayer of Petition*

*The vocabulary of supplication in the New Testament is rich in shades of meaning: ask, beseech, plead, invoke, entreat, cry out, even "struggle in prayer." Its most usual form, because the most spontaneous, is petition: by prayer of petition we express awareness of our relationship with God. We are creatures who are not our own beginning, not the masters of adversity, not our own last end.…Our petition is already a turning back to him.…Christian petition is centered on the desire and* search for the Kingdom to come, *in keeping with the teaching of Christ.*

## *III. Prayer of Intercession*

*Intercession is a prayer of petition which leads us to pray as Jesus did. He is the one intercessor with the Father on behalf of all men.…Intercession—asking on behalf of another—has been characteristic of a heart attuned to God's mercy.…In intercession, he who prays looks "not only to his own interests, but also to the interests of others," (Phil. 2:4) even to the point of praying for those who do him harm.*

## *IV. Prayer of Thanksgiving*

*Thanksgiving characterizes the prayer of the Church which, in celebrating the Eucharist, reveals and becomes more fully what she is.…As in the prayer of petition, every event and need can become an offering of thanksgiving.*

# Prayers from memory or memory in prayers?

*Saying a prayer from memory is the most universal way of praying....For many people, it is the only way of talking to God....Saying a prayer is easy and very educational because children do not know how to address God. They take their first steps with memorized prayers, since they put in their mouths what they should say.*

*(Translated from the Spanish)* Attributed to Francisco Jálics

We have a very old custom of teaching children to memorize prayers. In some cases the practice was somewhat exaggerated and turned into nonsense for children, who ended up learning prayers that were impractical even for adults. Remember, children will be able to learn by heart to the extent that the content is accessible to their mental development and maturity.

Some prayers, however, that are part of Christian life and of the Church's living memory could be learned by heart without forcing the children. It is also important to highlight the meaning of the prayers. The point is for these memorized texts to be interiorized and gradually understood in their depth so that they become a source of personal and communal Christian life. We should teach children to use their memory intelligently and creatively.

## *Younger children*

Younger children can learn short or ejaculatory prayers, though we need to ensure that such prayers are not childish or meaningless for later life.

It is always good to teach them phrases or sentences with a deep religious meaning, such as "Glory to God! Hallelujah! Yes, Lord! Here I am, Lord! Amen! Thank you, Lord! Forgive me, Lord! Sacred Heart of Jesus, I trust in you! May Jesus live in our hearts forever! Jesus, Mary, and Joseph, I give you my heart and soul!"

We may suggest very short prayers that children can finish themselves, such as "God, you are…my king…my creator…my best friend…powerful," and so forth. The Sign of the Cross, the Our Father, the Hail Mary, and the Glory Be should also be taught from a young age. Just remember to emphasize the inner attitude of prayer more than the memorization. The children will eventually memorize the prayers.

## *Age eight or nine*

By this time, children are beginning to have some abstract thought. We can now start teaching prayers such as the *Salve Regina*, the *Confiteor* (I Confess…), the *Gloria* (long version), and the *Creed* (Nicene and Apostles').

They can also learn some phrases from Scripture or the saints, such as, "Lord Jesus Christ, Son of David, have mercy on me, a sinner!" or "In the evening of life, we shall be judged on love" (Saint John of the Cross). Others include "Praised be Jesus Christ, may he be forever praised!" and "Remember that we are in the holy presence of God: we worship you, Lord!"

The purpose of memorizing prayers is to help us enter the presence of God, to dispose our hearts and minds to get in touch with God, our Father. Try to avoid letting recitation become merely mechanical.

It is important to keep in mind a prayer's deeper meaning, to pray it as calmly and intentionally as possible so that our words do not become a mindless repetition. If our prayers are recited with inner conviction and devotion, they acquire a deep meaning. For example, think of how many people have made the rosary a part of their lives and a way of communicating with God through the prayerful presence of the Virgin Mary.

> *The memorization of basic prayers offers an essential support to the life of prayer, but it is important to help learners savor their meaning.*
> Catechism of the Catholic Church, 2688

As we teach our children to pray, we should avoid the following errors, which are quite common:

- Reducing prayer to merely memorizing certain preestablished prayers.

- Focusing solely or too much on the prayer of petition. Experience shows that children easily lend themselves to the prayers of praise and thanksgiving.

- Choosing prayers that are suitable only for children. A child's prayer has to be truthful. Children's prayers that are only "true" for a certain time are inadequate.

- Forcing children to pray when they are not ready to do so. We cannot force anyone to pray. We can only invite and encourage them. We have to respect the child's own pace. Prayer should be an enjoyable experience, something that arises from within the heart.

- Praying for long intervals. Our prayer should be short and simple. As a rule, when we direct a prayer with children, it should not last more than a couple of minutes.

- Praying in a difficult or incomprehensible language. Many Christians have gotten used to praying in a religious and artificial language that they themselves do not understand. Consider the phrase, "Lord Jesus, cover us with your precious blood." What is a child going to imagine when hearing those words? *Are drops of blood falling from heaven? Will Jesus come with a bloody blanket to cover us?* We should at least clarify the scope and metaphors of the terms we use.

- Continuing the prayer when children become distracted or are causing trouble. When this happens, it is better to say "Amen" and finish the prayer. We can pick up the prayer again later in a quiet moment.
- Trying to get kids to pray "adult style" in a rigid and structured way. Children's prayers should be spontaneous, cheerful, and lack preestablished structures.
- Believing that introducing prayer to children is a woman's job and restricting it to bedtime. Introducing children to prayer is everyone's duty and can be done at any time. The whole family should participate.

To pray, children need:

- *An environment of trust.* Children need the assurance that they can trust those who are present.
- *Personal knowledge of God as our Father.* Children also need the assurance that God can be trusted. Children who think that God is far away or that the Lord is an old curmudgeon who only wants to punish them are not going to pray.
- *The opportunity to speak freely to the Lord.* This means telling God how we feel; sharing our joys, sorrows, and needs.
- *A variety of ways and methods.* In prayer, the time of concentration is even shorter because children cannot see the God to whom they are speaking.
- *Things to see, touch, do...*We also need to prepare visual and creative ways to introduce children to prayer.
- *A little time each day devoted to personal prayer.* When children really learn to pray, then we can tell them that they can talk to God every day, no matter where they are: at home, at school, in the car, and so forth.

# Psalms and children

*The psalms teach us how we must praise God and give us the right words.*

*(Translated from the Spanish)* Attributed to Saint Athanasius

Ancient peoples preserved traditions through legends, sayings, and songs passed on by word of mouth, as is the case with the psalms. The psalms are the highest expression of prayer in the Old Testament. They resonate with all kinds of people because they express the attitude that every person should have before God. Throughout the centuries, the Jewish people composed prayers to come before God with the most varied human emotions: fear, joy, gratitude, supplication, and praise.

The psalms are 150 of the most beautiful prayer hymns in existence. These wonderful prayers are recited day in and day out in churches, monasteries, homes, cathedrals, and chapels by saints and sinners, by people full of joy and gratitude, and by people torn by anxiety, fear, or remorse. They were written by various prophets, sages, and poets (Kings David and Solomon and the prophet Ezra, among others). They have been the favorite prayers of God's people for more than twenty-three centuries. The Israelites recited them long before Christ. Jesus and his apostles recited them, as did the Virgin Mary and the great saints of all time.

The Catholic Church—considering the psalms as inspired by the Holy Spirit—has made them its official prayer, expressed in the Liturgy of the Hours. Though the original words of the psalms have not changed, their meaning has been greatly enriched. In the New Covenant, the faithful praise and thank the God who revealed the secrets of his inner life and who rescued them with the blood of his Son and infused them with the Holy Spirit. In the liturgy, each psalm concludes with the Trinitarian doxology of the Glory be to the Father, and to the Son, and to the Holy Spirit.

## *The psalms and prayer*

The psalms are the song book that God's people—first the Jews, then the Church—have used to praise, pray, and give thanks. In short, they have been used for personal and communal prayer to God. These prayers were always sung. In fact, the word *psalm* means "hymn to be recited with music." In some cases, like the psalms of praise, the people danced and sang them to the accompaniment of many musical instruments.

The central theme of all the psalms is how good our God is, how powerful and very faithful, how kind to those who keep his Law, and how terrible to those who despise the divine commands. For the psalmists, the name of God was the sweetest and most lovely word human lips could utter.

The psalms, therefore, are an invitation to turn our lives into a prayer of trust and thanksgiving. In them we discover that we must present ourselves to God not as an "I" but as a "we," as a people united in prayer. They are true poems that raise the heart to God; they are life become prayer.

When a person gets used to praying the psalms slowly, few other prayers (except the Our Father and the Hail Mary) seem quite so beautiful as these ancient hymns, and few other prayers reach so deeply into the soul.

> *…A journey of hope. A window open to trust. A prayer full of human feelings. The Psalms, expressing the many situations of daily life lived in the light of faith, can be a great way to unite faith and life.*
>
> (*Translated from the Spanish*) Attributed to John Paul II

## *Praying the psalms with children*

It is important to tell children that as a boy, Jesus participated in the prayer of his people by singing and reciting the psalms. We can be sure that whenever we pray a psalm, we are repeating the same words Jesus memorized, recited, meditated on, and used to pray.

Scripture says that Jesus' family went on pilgrimage to the Temple in Jerusalem every year. (See Luke 2:41.) We can imagine the boy Jesus singing with the other children, and we can also imagine Mary and Joseph participating in the processions. As an adult, Jesus went on pilgrimage to Jerusalem and would often have joyfully sung:

> *I rejoiced when they said to me,*
> *"Let us go to the house of the LORD!"*
> *And now our feet are standing*
> *within your gates, Jerusalem.*

Psalm 122

And so, in many episodes of the gospels, we glimpse or contemplate Jesus singing or praying the psalms with devotion and conviction, as well as the entire Jewish people, as a way to communicate with God the Father. (See Mark 14:26.)

As with all of God's Word, we must be convinced that the psalms are also meant for children, and part of our task is to help children discover the beauty and power of the psalms, to enable them to make these ancient prayers their own.

Even the smallest children can pray the psalms. The first thing is to make sure they fully understand the words. In addition to clarifying the meaning of the words of the psalms, it is helpful to explain when and why they were written and at what times and on what occasions they were used. Essentially, we have to explain that the psalms are poetry and prayer.

Once they have grasped the psalms' context, children can gradually incorporate them into their prayers as an expression of their feelings and moods. In addition to choosing a translation that children can understand, I recommend taking the following methodological aspects into account:

- Recite the psalms in two groups and respond together, singing the chorus. (A boy or a girl reads the chorus and everyone repeats it. Each child reads a verse with conviction, and all answer in unison with the refrain.)
- Read the psalms with devotion. Have the children express or share what they understand of the psalm with a drawing or other form of artistic expression.
- In small groups, invent an appropriate stanza that has to do with the spirit and poetry of the psalm.
- Look for sung versions of the same psalm and establish similarities and differences.
- Explore the feelings that a psalm brings up and talk about the times we have felt the same in our lives.
- Choose a psalm and together invent a new chorus that summarizes it.
- Use different moments to incorporate psalms into the children's prayers.
- Analyze the meaning of different psalms and moments in life that may relate to them.
- Create gestures to accompany and reinforce the meaning of the psalms we are praying.
- Compare psalms and establish similarities and differences. Think together about when would be good times to pray them.

These are merely a few ideas for how to pray the psalms with children. The important thing is for the children themselves to incorporate and value them as a privileged form of prayer to God our Father. If the psalms have been used for centuries to approach God, they will certainly serve to bring children closer to the heart of God.

The following psalms are most suitable for children:

- 5 —Listen to me, Lord!
- 8 —God is wonderful!
- 18a —The voice of the Lord goes out to all the earth.
- 18b —Your Word, Lord, is the truth!
- 23 —Jesus is our good shepherd.
- 24 —Happy are the friends of God.
- 27 —God helps me, I shall not be afraid.
- 42 —My soul thirsts for God.
- 47 —Let us cry out to God with joy!
- 51 —When I have distanced myself from God.
- 63 —I thirst for God.
- 66 —Lord, the whole earth praises you!
- 96 —Let the heavens be glad and the earth rejoice!
- 98 —Sing a new song unto the Lord!
- 100 —Praise the Lord, all you creatures!
- 103 —God is good to us!
- 104 —Lord, send out your Spirit and renew the face of the earth!
- 117 —This is the day the Lord has made, Alleluia!
- 123 —To you, Lord, I lift my gaze.
- 135 —Great praise to God.
- 138 —Thank you, Lord, for your love!
- 139 —You know me, Lord!
- 147 —Glorify the Lord, Jerusalem!
- 150 —Glory to the Lord!

*We can say that the psalms serve to place in our heart and mouth the feelings and words of Jesus Christ himself, with whom we wish to identify ourselves.*

(*Translated from the Spanish*) Attributed to Benedict XVI

# The Lord's Prayer: Jesus' favorite prayer

*Go through all the prayers in the Scriptures. I do not think you will find anything that is not included in the Lord's Prayer.*
(*Translated from the Spanish*) Attributed to Saint Augustine

In the New Testament, the perfect model of prayer is found in Jesus' filial prayer. Often prayed in solitude, in secret, Jesus' prayer involves a loving adherence to the Father's will and an absolute confidence in being heard.

In this context, Jesus uses one of the most beautiful and profound prayers of all: the Our Father. When one of his disciples asks him how to pray (Luke 11:1), Jesus—as one who teaches with authority—entrusts his legacy to us in this prayer. The Lord's Prayer captures the essence of the Gospel. It summarizes and prioritizes the immense riches of prayer contained in sacred Scripture and the life of the Church.

Saint Augustine said the Lord's Prayer is the summary of the whole Gospel. The Lord's Prayer is the heart of the holy Scriptures and the center of the proclamation of the Good News.

The Our Father, the Hail Mary, and the Glory Be make up the heart of Jesus' legacy. And so it seems appropriate for children to learn them by heart at first. From a young age, children should not only be learning the Lord's Prayer, but have the right to receive an explanation of its meaning so as to live it with an ever-deepening joy and awareness.

An excellent way to teach children the Our Father is to examine the prayer line by line, explaining the concepts and how to live them, then praying over the content of each sentence with the children.

For example, I suggest taking the phrase *our Father*. What special considerations these two words evoke! It is enough just to think about what it means to call God "Father."

*God is our Father.* The Lord loves us as true sons and daughters. God gave us life. He gave us the world around us. God knows what we need…and so on.

*If God is our Father, we are all brothers and sisters.* We are all equal before God. As brothers and sisters, we must treat one another with love and respect. We are all united and responsible for our brothers and sisters…and so on.

You can continue in this manner with each sentence or phrase of the Our Father. All of this, in turn, can be accompanied by drawings, poems, songs, or any other catechetical resource that can help us go deeper with the children into the words Jesus left us. Of course, apart from our teaching efforts, the most important thing is for the children to perceive our disposition and fervor of heart when reciting the Lord's Prayer. We should do the same with the Hail Mary, the Glory Be, the Creed, and the other main Christian prayers.

*Our Father: that name inspires love, pleasure in prayer, and also the hope of receiving what we are going to ask…for how could he deny his children's prayer when he has already enabled them to be his children?*

(*Translated from the Spanish*) Attributed to Saint Augustine

## Praying the rosary

From the beginning of Christianity, the rosary has been one of the people of God's most widespread and beloved devotions, expressing unconditional love for the Virgin Mary, our beloved mother. The Virgin Mary loves it when we pray the rosary; it is one of her favorite prayers.

Rosary immediately calls to mind the image of a bouquet of roses or other flowers that we might give to someone we love. Praying the rosary is like bringing flowers to Mary. These flowers have a fragrance and beauty of their own, which is passed on to whoever gives and receives them.

The rosary is not a prayer of Christian initiation, but a point of arrival in the journey of faith. The rosary is not fully appreciated unless it is lived, unless it is prayed with the right interior disposition. We learn to love the rosary by praying it. The rosary is an easy and simple way for everyone to discover prayer.

The rosary is like a hidden treasure: we must work to find it, but once we do, it gives much joy to the heart and thus will not desire to leave it. This treasure can also be entrusted to children. When we pray, we are summarizing the Gospel of Jesus, the most important events in his life as seen in Mary's company.

## *Praying the rosary with children*

Although praying the rosary is a devotion traditionally used by adults, I am convinced that, with the necessary adaptations, the rosary is also a form of prayer that can help children approach Mary and, through her, God.

Because of its repetitive and monotonous nature, the rosary can be boring and even tedious for a child. We need to find ways to make it more accessible to young minds.

The first thing we should do is help the children discover the meaning of prayers of repetition. These prayers have to do with the internal rhythm of a person: they harmonize the person's breathing, senses, and heartbeat. In that sense, the rosary is a slow unfolding of the Hail Marys until they become part of the person praying. We don't have to finish the rosary quickly. It is preferable to pray fewer Hail Marys, but enjoy them more and pray them more meaningfully.

One of the first aspects to consider while praying with children is gradualism. Obviously, if we pray a complete rosary the first time, children will surely get bored and eventually abandon their attitude of prayer. With children, we have to look for various ways of praying the rosary so that they gradually learn to enjoy saying it without any pressure or obligation. This is accomplished by the contagious effect of the adults' enthusiasm and creativity.

*Some proposed strategies for praying the rosary with children*

- Start with just a few intense Hail Marys. Teach the children the meaning of the various mysteries of the rosary. Reflect on what each mystery is about, and go into its Gospel message. These early reflections may be accompanied by some aesthetic expression, such as a drawing, modeling, a story, representation or dramatization, images, and so forth.
- Pray a decade of the rosary with the kids, interspersing between each Hail Mary some allusion to the mystery being contemplated, such as an image that it suggests.
- Contemplate in each Hail Mary a different image of the Blessed Virgin's various titles (Tower of David, Mystical Rose), with a brief commentary on the origin of each invocation and what it means for us. Pray slowly, stopping to contemplate each image, her beauty, her face, her gestures, her signs, and so forth.
- Seat the children in a circle on the floor in a warm, welcoming, and softly lit room. Place an image of the Blessed Virgin in the center with a lighted candle, and have each child pray at least one Hail Mary aloud slowly and serenely. Have the children add their personal intentions as they pray.
- Try some creative variations on the rosary, like praying together until you come to the words, "Blessed is the fruit of thy womb, Jesus." At that point, have each child add a different invocation like the following:

> Holy Mary, Mother of the Church…
> Holy Mary, Mother of children…
> Holy Mary, who unties the knots in our hearts…
> Holy Mary, who cares for and protects us always…
> Holy Mary, you were always beside your Son…

All conclude the Hail Mary with "Pray for us sinners now and at the hour of our death. Amen."

- Children can invent different greetings to address the Blessed Virgin. For example, introduce the Hail Mary and replace the opening two words as suggested below:

  > God bless you, Mary…!
  > Good morning, Mary…!
  > Rejoice, Mary…!
  > Hello, Mary, how good you are…!
  > Hello, Mary, how beautiful you are…!

  After each child's greeting, all continue praying, "…full of grace, the Lord is with thee…" to finish the Hail Mary.

- Have the children make rosaries out of different materials either for their own use or to give to other people (relatives, other children, elderly people in a nursing home, and so forth). They enjoy giving them away. While making the rosaries, the kids can pray a Hail Mary, interspersed with a few songs, so all of that time becomes a moment of community prayer. It is always good to have an image of the Blessed Virgin to oversee the meeting.

It's simply a matter of using your imagination and of being confident in Mary's arms. It is she who is going to help make the rosary a path of spiritual growth with the children. What matters is our attitude of prayer, our spirit of prayer, our belief that the rosary is something beautiful. Then surely the kids will catch our enthusiasm.

# Chapter 2
# Praying With the Senses

*You shall love the Lord, your God, with all your heart, with all your being, with all your strength, and with all your mind.*
Luke 10:27

One of the risks of our culture and time is the division of the person. So we must stress that prayer is not just a matter of the intellect or even just of the emotions…but of the intellect, emotions, spirit, and body—our whole person. Prayer has to do with everything in us that is open to a relationship with God. It is about loving God with all our being.

It seems the only source of knowledge today, especially in the West, is through the intellect, through reason. This is a serious mistake that has often affected the realm of prayer. For many, prayer resembles reflective meditation. People do not realize that the senses can greatly help to tune us in to the things of God. They can especially prepare children to find their own way of prayer. We must fully integrate the body in prayer. Jesus himself often used his senses to proclaim and announce the Good News. Therefore it is important to highlight the use of our senses when teaching children to pray.

*The need to involve the senses in interior prayer corresponds to a requirement of our human nature. We are body and spirit, and we experience the need to translate our feelings externally. We must pray with our whole being to give all power possible to our supplication.*

*Catechism of the Catholic Church*, 2702

## Praying with the eyes: Knowing how to LOOK

*God looked at everything he had made, and found it very good.*
Genesis 1:31

The eyes and the gaze are an inexhaustible source of praise and prayer. We must gradually accustom children to taking a contemplative walk through the world around them.

We can ask them to take a silent stroll through familiar places, discovering the hidden beauties, the goodness of people and things—in a word, the loving presence of God who gave us all of creation. In that moment, we can inwardly thank God for all we can see with our eyes. Then we can share what we experienced and thank God, praying together. The children can have similar experiences.

The goal is to learn to look at others with the eyes of Jesus and to see him in others. This is a concrete way to recognize Jesus in our brothers and sisters. Jesus' gaze purifies the heart. The light of the countenance of Jesus enlightens the eyes of our heart and teaches us to see everything in the light of his truth and compassion for all humanity.

## Praying with the ears: Knowing how to LISTEN

*Mary kept all these things, reflecting on them in her heart.*

Luke 2:19

Prayer is active listening, that is, being open and attentive. In this sense, all the exercises that help us get in touch with our own body and feelings, without rejecting or rationalizing them, help pave the way for prayer. I cover this topic at greater length in Chapter 4.

Another way to pray is to listen attentively to those around us, to understand their real and deep needs and their life situation. Children can gradually learn to listen to others (at home, at school, with friends), and then pray for their needs.

## Praying with the hands: Knowing how to TOUCH

*What we looked upon and touched with our hands, concerns the Word of life—*

1 John 1:1

We are not used to perceiving all the good we can do with our hands. Hands are a powerful tool for personal communication. We must learn to value the role of our hands in our prayer life.

We can start with a simple exercise, like taking a fruit such as a banana with our eyes closed. Teach the children to perceive its texture, its roughness, its warmth or coolness. After a while, have them begin to peel it slowly, so as not to "hurt" it. First reconnect with its shape, texture, and smell, and then eat it slowly, savoring every bite. When finished, thank God for the miracle of beauty, flavor, food, and color within this and every fruit.

Other exercises can include modeling, using papier mâché, clay, salt dough, or any other moldable material. In silence or accompanied by soft music, put the children in a circle. Divide the material and guide them so they perceive the softness and pliability of the clay, which they can mold with their hands. In the end, have them all share their experience and praise God for all the gifts they have received.

Another step is to consider how we use our hands as a means of communication. Show how all the gestures we can make in a group (some of which are developed later when we talk about sacred signs) bring us closer to others and help us better communicate with God.

## Praying with the mouth: Knowing how to TASTE and SPEAK

*It is not what enters one's mouth that defiles that person; but what comes out of the mouth.*

Matthew 15:11

We can also give children a number of experiences to make them more conscious of enjoying the taste of food. We need to teach them to take the time to delight in every meal, compare its taste with others, enjoy every taste, and praise God for the variety and exquisite flavors he gave us in nature.

Perhaps the most difficult issue for humanity is to avoid hurting others with our words. In this sense, everything that helps us to be aware of this situation brings us closer to God. Not only do we have to help children internalize the use of *good words,* telling them, "Thank you…Have a good day…Please…You're welcome…Sorry… Excuse me," but we must also include specific exercises to become aware of those times when we hurt others.

For example, during a time of prayer, we might think about those we may have hurt by our words, pray for them, keep them in mind, and then ask for forgiveness.

Children can gradually become aware of all they can say to God with their lips: praise, thanksgiving, petition, and so forth.

# Praying with the nose: Knowing how to SMELL

*For we are the aroma of Christ for God among those who are being saved.*

2 Corinthians 2:15

As with taste, we can have a number of olfactory experiences. Along with taste, the sense of smell is probably one of the least developed (at least for those abiding in cities). These exercises can be similar to those of taste.

By closing our eyes, we can perceive different smells and aromas. We can also try recognizing various fragrances. The point is to make children increasingly aware of the sense of smell and praise God for all we can do with it.

Thus we have ventured into how to develop the senses in prayer, or rather, how to pray using the senses. Children enjoy these experiences more than adults suspect. They enjoy them even more when they are combined and when they express them in a group to praise God.

# Chapter 3
# Praying Through Gestures, Singing, and Drawing

*The catechesis of children, young people, and adults aims at teaching them to meditate on the Word of God in personal prayer, practicing it in liturgical prayer, and internalizing it at all times in order to bear fruit in a new life.*

*Catechism of the Catholic Church,* 2688

Gestures, singing, and drawing are some of the ways in which children pray. It is through these activities that we will recognize and assist them to achieve true moments of prayer.

Children not only enjoy but express themselves in a complete and total way through song, gesture, and drawing. Their whole personality resonates with and is expressed through the senses, even more so when they sing and make gestures.

# Gestures

*Contrary to what happens with the adult, the gesture is not the child's projection of an idea or a feeling that tends to externalization. Rather, it is the means by which the idea or feeling enters his consciousness.*

(*Translated from the Spanish*) Lubienska de Lenval

For children, gestures are much more meaningful than words. Gestures allow children to express what words cannot say. For example, a child will express praise to God much more profoundly by waving at God with her arms to accompany the words "I praise God" than if she just says the words alone.

Most kids need gestures much more than words to express themselves. For them, if the whole body or parts of it are not involved, communication seems incomplete. This is all the more true in prayer.

It is one thing to say we're happy because Jesus loves us; it's another to dance around a statue of Jesus, singing with our whole being, "I have a friend who loves me."

Obviously kids not only enjoy it more when their whole body expresses what they feel, but this expression makes them feel more deeply what they say. We must ensure that children live the religious gestures they make. Unfortunately, routine or a lack of knowledge can eventually nullify the meaning of gestures that were once very valuable.

Here I propose a list and a brief explanation of the sacred gestures commonly used in our personal prayers or community celebrations to help us better communicate with God.

- **Sign of the Cross:** This is the sign of salvation, since Jesus redeemed us on the cross. It is the sign of Christ. It should be made slowly, broadly, and carefully. When we make it, we put ourselves in God's presence for any and all life situations.

- **Sign of the Cross (long)**: We make three crosses, slowly and ceremoniously, first on the forehead, then on the lips, and finally on the chest. At the same time, we say,

  + O Lord, open my mind;
  + O Lord, open my lips;
  + Open my heart to listen and proclaim your Word.

  This Sign of the Cross is used before the proclamation of the Gospel, replacing the previous (short) version. Therefore, only this one should be made.

- **Standing**: When something or someone important is coming, standing means being willing and ready to respond.

- **Kneeling:** Before the greatness and holiness of God, we kneel to express our smallness, our humility, our praise for the God who loves us and gave us life. Kneeling indicates that the heart is bowing with deep respect for God.

- **Sitting:** This is the attitude of openness to listen carefully to another or to the Word of God.

- **Inclining the head:** Indicates reverence or a greeting to God. We use this gesture when we pass in front of the altar.

- **Bowing**: Like the previous gesture, bowing shows adoration and respect in the presence of God.

- **Genuflection:** The right knee touches the ground, the left knee is bent, and the head is bowed. It indicates greeting and worship, especially in front of the Blessed Sacrament in the tabernacle.

- **Striking the chest:** A sign of penance. Repentance is manifested through a soft blow to the chest with a closed fist. It symbolizes hitting the doors of our interior world to call us to see God and return to him.

- **Standing with open arms:** The soul opens fully to God as a sign of joy, praise, jubilation, and thanksgiving.
- **The sign of peace:** The sign of peace not only means we are reconciled to others but expresses the hope that God will flood us with his peace.
- **Hands:** In a particular way, the face and hands are the soul's mirror and instruments. After the face, hands are the most expressive part of the body. With them we can make different gestures that have different meanings:

    —**Hands together:** expresses the union of the whole person who is oriented toward God on high.

    —**Interlaced fingers:** faced with a stressful situation or deep grief, interlaced fingers express the need for unity and inner strength as the person asks God for help.

    —**Open hands extended upward:** expresses the attitude of receiving something, of receiving God; in some cases it can mean imploring help from above.

    —**Holding hands:** a sign of unity and of an affectionate bond uniting those making the gesture.

    —**Laying on of hands:** hands extended down over another's head signifies the transmission of the force and the power of the Spirit who is poured out in us.

    —**Clapping for God:** expresses approval and joy over everything we have received.

- **Blessing:** Only God can bless and does so through his ministers. His almighty love is aimed at the hearts of his creatures. From God's hand flows the holy and good strength that makes us grow. God gives himself. Only the Lord can bless people. When objects are blessed, God is blessing the people who will use them.

- **Processional entrance:** Expresses the march of the people of God, a journey they make together as a people to the Father.
- **Taking grace:** This happens when we approach an image, touch it, and make the Sign of the Cross. We ask saints to intercede with God so that the Lord will shed his grace on the one who implores it.
- **Kissing or blowing kisses to an image:** These are ways of expressing affection and reverence. It is important to help children understand the relative value of images.
- **Bringing flowers or gifts:** Expresses affection, remembrance, and thoughts about the other. This is especially true when it comes to the Virgin Mary.
- **Candles:** The lighted candle represents the presence of the risen Christ, especially the paschal candle. Light, which gives form, color, and meaning to things, is a sign of life, a sign of God.
- **Holy water:** Water is full of mystery. It is clear, simple, purifying, comforting, and powerful all at the same time. Life flows forth from it. When we make the Sign of the Cross, dipping our fingers in holy water with proper interior disposition, our venial(or small) sins are forgiven.

It is very important to seek out and explain the meaning of the gestures we make. We should always take a moment to reflect on the sacred gestures we use so that we internalize them and make them intentionally.

We must demand great authenticity and sincerity from ourselves and from children so that we do not perform empty gestures without the right internal attitudes. And we should always make the gestures with the children. That's how we pass on the "bug" of enthusiasm that helps kids grow in their faith. Sometimes we can create gestures with the kids; the important thing is to help them express their love for God.

Any religious gesture used in prayer and lived with intensity will help us establish greater communication with God, our Lord.

## Singing

*Singing is characteristic of one who loves;*
*singing is praying twice.*

(*From the Spanish*) Attributed to Saint Augustine

Singing is an intense form of expression that is verbal, poetic, and musical at the same time. It is one of the most complete forms of human expression and perhaps one of the best ways to worship and communicate with God.

Song has a very important place in a child's prayer. Along with gestures, it is one of the forms of expression that children enjoy and get into most. Songs reach so deeply into the hearts of children that they often remember them for a lifetime.

Religious songs are an important educational, recreational, and pastoral resource. Singing should be a daily and permanent part of children's catechesis. I believe that the inclusion of song in the catechesis of children is an excellent methodological choice since, in practice, it is a "sung catechesis."

Especially when we add songs with gestures. This "magical" fusion of singing and gestures generates a response in children that we cannot even imagine and whose educational power is difficult to fully grasp. Those who have had the experience know that children enjoy few things more than "singing with the whole body," or combining gesture, song, and prayer.

A creative catechist can make up songs with the children and choose the gestures that go best with the songs. Of course, as always, the catechist will not only have to do these gestures but must live and sing with full intensity.

*Some notes on singing with children*

- We need to take special care with the content of the songs because of how they make such a mark on a child's heart. We should avoid teaching corny, silly simplifications that lack any poetry or indulge theological nonsense.
- The content must be simple, deep, and accessible to the child's understanding. I recommend explaining the words first.
- A song addressed to the Lord must be differentiated from other common songs by its form and by the way we sing it.
- The melody should be suited to a child's age. It should be cheerful, fast, short, rhythmic, simple, repetitive, and easy to remember.
- If possible, a good portion of the songs should be accompanied with gestures that reinforce the content without being silly or ridiculous.
- The lyrics and melody should fit the context of the catechetical topic.
- We must use creativity, ingenuity, and incentive to get kids to "live" the songs dedicated to God.
- The kids are more aware of the song itself than of the way it is sung by the catechist (they are not demanding judges but rather an audience eager to sing and learn a new song). So we can move and sing with a certain calm, even if we make mistakes.
- If you do not feel capable of singing, you could use a music player, although that is not the best option.

Many parents would like to have copies of songs to sing with their children at home. Catechists and teachers need to know which ones to recommend.

We can use tapes or CDs, but we should not rely on them too much. Many beautiful songs end up "stale" because we repeat them on every occasion.

Prayer through singing and singing in prayer are two sides of the same coin. The deepest experiences of prayer for the psalmists, saints, and Christians are inextricably joined to songs of praise and thanksgiving. Throughout the life of the Church, song has been a privileged expression of prayer.

In children, the need to combine singing with prayer is much deeper and responds much better to their condition as children. From there, we must not by any means miss the enormous richness of song in the believer's prayer, catechesis, and faith life.

Thanks to God and to the work of many catechists, musicians, and poets, the repertoire of religious songs for kids is increasing day by day. We need to keep up with them and spread them around so that others can use them.

These directions are only a guide to the use of religious song in catechesis and prayer.

Of course, the only way to learn to sing songs with the kids is to sing along with them, and only those who have been through this beautiful experience can realize its immense value for catechesis.

## Drawing

*We need to contemplate the beauty of the Father and impregnate our soul with it.*

(*Translated from the Spanish*) Attributed to Saint Gregory of Nyssa

Drawing, or artistic expression in general, is one form of expression that kids get most excited about. Children like to draw and frequently apply and share much of themselves when they set out to make a piece of art.

Plastic expression mobilizes a child so that his or her whole being is absorbed by the activity, producing as much pleasure and dedication as playing games.

Such enthusiasm could be used to channel a moment of prayer so that pleasure, devotion, and prayer are closely linked. This resource should be used regularly in catechesis, though without tiring or exhausting the kids as this will restrict their creative capacity.

Moreover, anything that helps kids develop their creative capacity helps them participate indirectly in God's creation. Every creative act is a participation in creation. The pursuit of beauty is, in essence, the seeking of God.

In children, the experience of faith and the expression of faith are inextricably linked. For them, activities of religious expression are a way of reliving what they just experienced in catechesis. That is, if the child has a faith experience, he relives it and internalizes it when he can express it through his own creation. Also, when he is expressing faith, he is having an experience of faith. It is a process that constantly reinforces itself.

Making a drawing for God to the rhythm of tranquil music can become a moment of quiet prayer. Using these drawings to express our needs, our gratitude, or simply what we want to say or tell God is another way for all of us to express ourselves.

Whenever we draw, we should add specific catechetical content to the drawing. Insofar as it is possible, children should include themselves, their friends, family, Jesus, and so on in the drawing. We should not create any stereotyped image of God, much less correct the kids on this point. However, we can encourage their drawing and creativity through suggestions.

For example, we can stimulate their creativity through the reading of a biblical text. With paper in front of them and their materials ready, have youngsters close their eyes after hearing the story and imagine the scene: how the characters are dressed, what the weather is like, what sounds and noises they imagine in the scene, what the characters are saying to one another, what Jesus is saying, and what their attitude is. "I imagine my friends, my family, and so on within the scene. What colors best express what I imagined?" With suggestions and questions like these, we can guide children to make their drawing a prayer. Then we open our eyes and, with the joy of knowing that we are drawing for God, we get down to business.

Clearly we are not evaluating the quality or technique of the drawing but trying to make it a means of approaching God.

After the experience, the children can take the pictures home or to a Liturgy of the Word and offer them to God.

# Chapter 4
# Introduction to Silence

*Prayer is not only mental prayer, in my opinion, but a matter of friendship, of frequently spending time alone with the one who we know loves us. Contemplation seeks out my soul's beloved, that is, Jesus, and in him, the Father.*
(*Translated from the Spanish*) Attributed to Saint Teresa of Jesus

## The world without silence

Our world today, especially in large cities, seems to have declared silence "Public Enemy Number 1." Sounds and noises invade our lives to the point that it's difficult to find places of silence. Households, squares, roads, streets, even unpopulated areas are continually disturbed by noise.

Radio, television, newspapers, film, computers—everything fills us with noise, music, images, and words. This "culture of noise" is so embedded and internalized in humanity that we are often unable to get away from its influence.

Many people cannot be home alone in silence. They need to turn on the radio or television to "feel accompanied," even though they are not watching or listening to the program!

All this reality or "culture of noise" only conceals or covers other realities that are far more profound and disturbing: the lack of interiority or the prevailing superficiality, the fear of being alone with ourselves, the absence of any transcendent meaning in life, the denial of God…the list is very long.

We only know that human persons both need and run from silence. People find themselves alone, and instead of learning to walk comfortably within silence, they pretend it doesn't exist.

## Silence and the mystery of God

Getting initiated into silence is a journey, a process that continues throughout our lifetime. It becomes an ongoing exercise to draw closer to ourselves, to our brothers and sisters, and to God.

Silence is a release, an inner liberation. Making silence in our lives means developing our interiority, "growing within," inwardly predisposing ourselves to meet with the absolute—in a word, to prepare for prayer.

Spiritual silence is an intuition of God. For us, silence expresses a certain intuition of the mystery. Spiritual silence and personal prayer are almost synonymous. Personal prayer is nothing other than an attentive ear, an open mind, a silent listening to God's presence. Being quiet means making the senses attentive to the absolute.

## Biblical silence

Silence has two different connotations in Scripture: the silence of God and that of human beings.

### God's silence

In the *Old Testament*, God appears as the Holy One, the Other, the Unreachable. Therefore, his presence is permanent but fleeting, unknowable. God maintains a long silence:

"I cry to you, but you do not answer me; I stand, but you take no notice" (Job 30:20).

(Yahweh speaks) "For a long time I have kept silent, I have said nothing, holding myself back" (Isaiah 42:14).

"Whom did you dread and fear…? Am I to keep silent?" (Isaiah 57:11).

"Can you hold back, LORD, after all this? Can you remain silent, and afflict us so severely?" (Isaiah 64:11).

"To you, LORD, I call; my Rock, do not be deaf to me, do not be silent toward me, so that I join those who go down to the pit" (Psalm 28:1).

"Why is my pain continuous, my wound incurable, refusing to be healed? To me you are like a deceptive brook, waters that cannot be relied on!" (Jeremiah 15:18).

"Why, then, do you gaze on the faithless in silence while the wicked devour those more just than themselves?" (Habakkuk 1:13).

"Now to him who can strengthen you, according to my gospel and the proclamation of Jesus Christ, according to the revelation of the mystery kept secret for long ages" (Romans 16:25).

In the *New Testament*, God breaks his silence by becoming the Word in his Son Jesus. Jesus is the Word of God made flesh, the Word Incarnate. Human beings must then listen and predispose themselves to embody the Word in their lives.

## *Human silence*

Human silence becomes prayer. In the Bible, silence has vital connotations that people today do not always grasp. Speaking of silence in the Bible means speaking of openness, receptivity, and acceptance.

In silence, human beings become attentive to the presence of the Word of God, the Word who is God. Spiritual silence is the loving dialogue between a creature and his or her Creator, of children with their Father. This dialogue is lifelong, and the person gradually grows in his commitment until it makes us into a new creation.

It is in this sense that the biblical texts are oriented. Some refer directly to silence, while others refer to it implicitly. The basic attitude of the believer is the same: openness.

The following texts on silence can be useful for catechesis with children and also for personal reflection:

**From the Old Testament**

- God speaks to Moses (Exodus 3:1–5): In the silence of the countryside, God speaks and Moses listens.
- Moses speaks to God in the tabernacle as to a friend (Exodus 33:7–11): In these passages, Moses speaks to God in the tent and in the silence of the desert. God speaks to Moses face-to-face, as any person would speak to a dear friend.
- God's call to Samuel (1 Samuel 3:1–10): God speaks to Samuel's heart in the silence of the night.
- The prophet Elijah encounters God (1 Kings 19:9–14): Elijah meets God in the gentle breeze.
- When God visits, a hush falls over the land (Habakkuk 2:20, Isaiah 41:1; Zechariah 2:17, Psalm 76:9; Revelation 8:1); once it has come, the silence of fear or respect is a sign of human worship (Lamentations 2:10; Exodus 15:16).
- "For when peaceful stillness encompassed everything and the night in its swift course was half spent, Your all-powerful word from heaven's royal throne leapt into the doomed land" (Wisdom 18:14–15).

- "The mind of the wise appreciates proverbs, and the ear that listens to wisdom rejoices" (Sirach 3:29).

**From the New Testament**

- Mary listened to the angel in silence (Luke 1:26–38): The eternal Word became flesh in her reception of this silence.
- Mary pondered all these things in her heart (Luke 2:19).
- Jesus sought out the silence and solitude of the night to talk to his Father (Luke 5:16, 6:12, 9:18, 11:1; Matthew 14:23; Mark 1:35).
- Jesus was transfigured in the presence of his Father (Luke 9:28–29; Matthew 17:1–9; Mark 9:2–10).
- Jesus prayed in the solitude of the Mount of Olives (Luke 22:39–45).
- Jesus taught us to speak to God alone (Matthew 6:6; Luke 2:19, 51).

# Types of silence

Before analyzing the various techniques of initiation into silence, we should make a distinction between two types of silence: passive and active.

## *Passive, physical, or external silence*

This silence consists in the absence of audible noise. The mere absence of noise or sound is enough to achieve this type of silence.

It is external, without the child's participation. Anyone can achieve passive silence by imposing an outside order or discipline. Externally there is silence but not necessarily within the children.

We can see this when we oblige a group of children to keep silent by threatening them with reprisals if they do not remain silent and still. When we have gotten them to be completely quiet, we exit the room, leaving them alone. The pressure will immediately give way and the silence will immediately disappear. It is a silence imposed without any participation from the children.

Passive silence is like a vacuum to be filled. When teaching children about silence, external silence is useless; we have to help them achieve inner silence.

### *Active, internal, or spiritual silence*

This type of silence consists in developing an attentive presence. It is achieved with the children's personal and spontaneous participation. It is not a vacuum; rather, it is something that fills and enriches us, which seeks to place all the senses in a receptive attitude of listening.

Active silence is internal and is achieved with the full participation of the person being catechized. This requires helping the children use their senses and imagination to observe and care about the people and things around them.

As they are educated in the active practice of silence, children begin to become more aware of reality. As we move forward, we discover that as children experience active silence, they go from attention and openness to concrete and tangible realities to an openness to the absolute God whom they cannot see.

Silence is one of love's most privileged expressions. Isn't communion between two people expressed in the rhythmic alternation of silences and words?

Silence is a release. Being silent frees us to be open to the Lord and others. Being silent helps us to walk toward and encounter the absolute, with and in God.

## Chapter 5
# Introducing Children to Silence

*Contemplative prayer is* silence, *the "symbol of the world to come" or "silent love." Words in this kind of prayer are not speeches; they are like kindling that feeds the fire of love. In this silence, unbearable to the "outer" man, the Father speaks to us his incarnate Word, who suffered, died, and rose; in this silence the Spirit of adoption enables us to share in the prayer of Jesus.*

Catechism of the Catholic Church, 2717

Starting out in silence is a journey, a process that is achieved gradually throughout life. It is a task that is part of ongoing catechesis. Helping kids to "be quiet" is not just about guiding them from the outside, but about achieving silence along with them.

The process may be difficult at first. In part, it may be because we ourselves are not accustomed to active silence. We should not be surprised if our first attempts are disappointing. The key to helping children enjoy or achieve this silence is persistence and gradualism.

It is very important to respect a child's pace. This is not a matter of imposing silence, but of helping children to create or achieve their own silence. Every catechist should know how to discover and contribute whatever elements help children encounter their interiority. The catechist and the children must adapt to the method.

When children are actively silent, their senses are stilled. For them, the absence of noise and motion is an unusual state that prepares them to perceive something different from everything else: the mysterious presence of God.

Any act of religious life requires special recollection. All prayer should be preceded by calm, a sort of vestibule of silence and concentration.

Every initiation into silence is a way of introducing prayer. Silence alone is not enough if it does not lead to an encounter with God. Every initiation into silence must eventually lead to a personal encounter with God, that is, to prayer. If this is not achieved, the entire catechetical effort is in vain and we would merely be doing relaxation and mental-concentration exercises.

The point of this whole process is to bring children to God. It's about helping them get the taste for prayer and come to experience a loving encounter with the Father. Without silence there is no prayer, but silence is meaningless without prayer.

## Practical considerations

When learning silence, it is very important to have the right atmosphere. The following should be taken into account:

- Find a proper place, like a warm or cozy room away from noise, that is appropriately prepared (carpets, pillows, subdued lighting, and so forth). If you do not have a suitable place, try to adapt a spot in the classroom at a suitable time.

- Take the moment into account. We not only have to consider the child's reality (for example, initiation into silence should not be tried when the kids are all riled up) but the reality outside the classroom as well (other classes in session, recreation, other church or school groups coming and going, and so forth).

- Once we have found the right place and time to pray with the children, it is best to keep it fixed. When children are familiar with the time and place for prayer, they are less distracted and take less time to get into an atmosphere of prayer.
- The catechist's or parent's voice, gestures, posture, and body all play an important role. We must carefully watch our tone, volume, gestures, and facial expressions. The catechist/parent must be the first one to create silence.
- Since it is a gradual process, introduction into silence should not be limited to the first meetings, but should be repeated again and again throughout the year.

The silence and peace of churches are full of meaning for children. It should be noted that:

- Children are already familiar with the church.
- If the church is very large, it would be best to meet within the most appropriate place for meditation (cushions can be arranged in front of the tabernacle or elsewhere).
- However, the church is not always the ideal place for teaching silence due to the possible distractions (many images, people walking around, a very large space, and so forth).
- It's not about keeping them quiet the whole time but about fostering an inner attitude that is then expressed exteriorly.
- It is very important to respect the moments of silence and interiority that the child or children will spontaneously show.

# Helpful techniques

One of the fundamental tasks of catechesis is to teach us to pray.

*Communion with Jesus Christ leads the disciples to assume the attitude of prayer and contemplation which the Master himself had. To learn to pray with Jesus is to pray with the same sentiments with which he turned to the Father: adoration, praise, thanksgiving, filial confidence, supplication and awe for his glory.*

General Directory for Catechesis, 1997, 85

I propose here a number of possibilities for teaching children silence. Many are techniques drawn from experience. They are not intended to be comprehensive—far from it. They come from my catechesis with children, from courses, from the experience of other catechists, from books I've read, and so forth.

Each catechist may change, add, or create new and original methods. These ideas are meant to be read, adapted, and used in whatever way is most helpful.

The proposals are sorted by age and degrees of complexity, although the order is only a guideline that can be used at different times of the year. Some are designed for younger children, while others can be used for later ages with the necessary adaptations.

Clarification: not all of the chosen methods contain catechetical content. Many of them are meant to be used just as steps to prepare the way for deeper techniques.

- Enter the room on tiptoe with "soft slippers" and settle in without a sound. Or enter like an astronaut in space, a character in a slow-motion film, or a deep-sea diver.

- Take a "journey" through outer space. Close your eyes, wear a spacesuit, board the craft, light the engines—all in absolute silence.

- Scream silently, gesturing and shouting "full force" but without making any sounds or noise. It's like mimicking a great shout.
- Create a "silence campaign" where you do everything quietly, using mimes.
- Bring in "Mr. Silence" by opening the door or window and calling for him to come in. When he arrives, he can only enter the room if there is silence. Any noise or sound "scares him." The game is repeated as many times as necessary until "Mr. Silence" is settled in the room.
- I am the "king of my body." I give orders to my body and it always obeys me. You can also give orders to the body of another king who obeys at a distance, all in silence.
- Play the "king of silence." The teacher presents the game in a low voice (the kids sit in a circle):

  *"I'm the king of silence. My subjects never make noise. To become one of my princes or princesses, you have to be able to get up and move without a sound. When we make a great silence, I'll point to one of you, who will rise without making any noise, and walk toward me. If you think you did well, tell me by signs and making a deep bow. Then you can become a 'prince.' If you made noise, we'll raise our arms and you will have to return to your place."*

  The game is completed as everyone changes places. There may be several orders: walk backward, hop on one foot, and so forth.
- Have a student leave the room while the others watch. The catechist changes something from its place or changes something about his or her wardrobe. The child should return and look in silence until he or she discovers the change.

- With their backs to the group or blindfolded, the children should try to recognize different noises or sounds the teacher or a classmate is making with different types of instruments.
- Pat the bench, starting out hard and very noisily, and then doing it more and more softly until not a sound is heard.
- Have the children close their eyes and turn on their "inner TV," imagining scenes suggested by the catechist or teacher. They can visualize all kinds of stories and situations. It is important to make room for the children's imagination and gradually increase the moments they spend with open, silent minds.
- Focus on some rhythmic and easy bodily exercises, such as rhythmic gymnastics, "balancing" on a bench or other object, or jumping over various obstacles in silence or to soft music.
- March in a line without making any noise. You can add other skills: arms crossed, one foot in front of the other, one arm outstretched and the other on a classmate's shoulder, and so on.
- Perform different rhythmic applauses, always ending in a long silence.
- Tell stories with mime. One child narrates a fact using only mime, and the others try to interpret it. Then they change roles.
- Do different types of mimes along with the kids and have them repeat the gestures "in parallel" and in silence.
- Play "charades" depicting a scene from the Bible, a parable of Jesus, an important event in the lives of the saints or patrons.
- Do a mime show, either live or on video. Do the mime techniques with the kids.
- Put on soft music and have the children lie down. While speaking very quietly, have them relax every part of their body until they reach a deep silence (at the end, turn off the music or turn it down until it is almost inaudible).

- Work in silence to the sound of calm and gentle music. Draw to the beat of the music. I suggest using instrumental music without major fluctuations, such as Baroque-period music, Andean instrumental music, or the entire range of electroacoustics and relaxation music.

- Sing an appropriate song and complete the last stanza, repeating the final melody until the song becomes inaudible, silently lip-synching the words.

- Have the children sing a song in their heads, eyes closed. When finished, the kids raise their hands. Repeat until everyone finishes at the same time. You can start, humming the song with your lips closed.

- Noises from far and near. It is good to do this exercise several times and gradually.

  **First step:** Children are invited to take a walk on the patio, on the sidewalk, on the terrace of the school or parish. During the short walk, children will silently listen and try to hear as many sounds and noises as possible. (You can also do it directly from the classroom without taking a walk.)

  Back in the room or classroom, ask the children to comment on the noises they heard during the walk. If they are tired, you can get them to relax by clapping along to a song, or leave this part of the step for another meeting (in this case, you'll remind them of what they did in this meeting).

  **Second step:** Ask the children to sit with arms folded on the table, resting their heads on their arms and closing their eyes. Tell them to ignore the noises coming from outside the classroom. Instruct the children to focus only on the sounds inside the room or classroom. It is important to be patient and let them take their time. Then have them describe what they heard. Include another song and/or clapping.

**Third step:** If they are tired, ask the children to go back to their former position. You can tell them, "We are going to forget about the noise outside and inside the classroom and focus all our efforts on listening to the noises and sounds within our own bodies. This must be the moment of greatest silence. If they don't achieve it, be patient and try it in other sessions. It is astonishing to note that children can come to express things like, "I heard my blood," "I felt my heart," "I heard my veins" or "my breathing."

- Don't forget to teach kids to breathe rhythmically and slowly, making breathing a form of prayer. Breathing not only connects with the body, it also connects the conscious and unconscious (since breathing occurs unconsciously but can also be controlled consciously). It's about learning to breathe rhythmically, slowly, and calmly, with the right interior disposition.

- Create silence for others. For example: when walking into a store, I can keep silence for someone I love. When traveling by bus, I can offer a moment of silence for someone I have trouble getting along with. If I have trouble falling asleep, I can calmly offer it to the Lord for people who are ill, and so forth.

- Make the most of the moments nature gives us to be totally absorbed, contemplating in silence, such as watching a sunset, the top of a mountain, the open sea. At such times, deliberately make a long contemplative silence. Do not pass up these types of encounters when you are in touch with nature: day trips, retreats, meetings, camps, and so forth.

- Do not neglect visits to churches, chapels, or other holy places, and encourage children to pray with you in silence.

- At all times of prayer, always include a space of inner silence, a space for personal and silent prayer, without hurry or pressure.

- Use your imagination as a form of prayer. This is a very effective remedy. You may take a biblical scene, a parable, or an event from Jesus' life. Then sit down, close your eyes, be quiet and relax, and read the biblical text. Children are guided to imagine the place, the arrangement of things, the location of the people, the colors, the flavors, the smells.

  Each one tries to reconstruct the biblical scene as he or she sees fit. Sometimes we can even re-create or imagine a dialogue with Jesus—his words, our answer—so the children can have an imaginary encounter with Jesus. The important thing is not to lose the spirit of prayer and to keep in mind that what we are experiencing is a fictional situation that only seeks to help put us in the presence of God.

- Get kids used to turning to personal prayer and silence to thank, to ask, to praise at the various times that come up during the day, the week, in different areas, and so forth.

- Remind and guide children so that, before praying at night or at any other time, they perform some exercise of silence.

- At home, before blessing the food, it would be very good to reserve a moment of silent prayer for the whole family.

These exercises give us an idea as to how to begin introducing children to silence. It's a matter of imagination, creativity, and finding silence before God. With time, those who integrate silence into their daily lives will learn to naturally crave it, for in this space God speaks and peace is found.

With these simple techniques, we will put our students on the path of silence, on the way of prayer. Lest we forget, prayer is primarily the result of the grace and love of God for us. These techniques would be in vain if God did not love us and if the Holy Spirit did not accompany us on our journey to the Father.

# Chapter 6

# A Place for Prayer

*He who unites prayer to works and works to prayer prays continually. Only then can the principle of continuous prayer be livable.*

(*Translated from the Spanish*) Attributed to Origen

In many schools, especially kindergarten and preschools and now also in some parishes, we find rooms that have special places called "departments," "workshops," "nooks," or simply "corners." We find the kitchen corner, the carpentry corner, the doll corner, the music room, the parish hall, and so forth.

Through corners or areas especially intended for a particular use, a child puts his mind and body in order. The habits and customs of a special nook or corner help a child discover that there is an order, a habit, a certain behavior for each place and time. Such corners help strengthen the space-time dimension in children.

Just as we have a designated place for work, play, and rest, it is important to have a specific place for prayer. Are not the churches in our large cities a "little corner," an oasis of calm and tranquility where we can pray?

But we must find the right time and place for the children to feel motivated to pray and get in touch with God.

## The prayer corner

The best place to pray is in a chapel or church. The atmosphere of silence and recollection, dim lighting, religious images, and the presence of the Blessed Sacrament in the tabernacle all lead the believer to immerse oneself in an atmosphere of prayer and contemplation.

However, a chapel or church is not always the best place to introduce children to prayer because of its size, distance, or constant use—unless it has a small chapel set apart and available for that purpose.

In my experience, the ideal would be to have a special room dedicated to this purpose near the place where catechism lessons are taught. This room should be a special place in the school or parish. It has to be warm, with little outward visibility (windows can be covered with cellophane), and with a rug or pillows for children to sit on the floor.

Place an image of Jesus, a Bible, the Easter candle, and some flowers on a small table with a white tablecloth in a prominent place in the room, creating a kind of catechetical lounge-chapel where kids can sense a different atmosphere the moment they enter.

I realize the idea of having a room exclusively for catechesis is very ambitious and not always possible. That's where the alternative of having a "prayer corner" in the classroom comes in. Having a prayer corner in the classroom allows several catechists to work at the same time. It's also a great advantage not to have to change locations every time.

It would also be a good idea for each family to have a place or an area dedicated to prayer, as our elders once did.

# Characteristics of the prayer corner

We must respect certain conditions for the prayer corner (or Jesus nook) to gradually "enter" the children's lives and become something sacred, something set apart especially for God. To set up the prayer corner, we should keep the following points in mind:

## *The place*

- One of honor: set apart, clean, always in order
- A low-traffic area with easy access
- Different: not used for other purposes
- Cheerful and bright

## *Images*

Experience shows the choice of images is very important. It is necessary to have an image of Jesus (since he is the center of catechesis). On occasion, it may be replaced with an image of the Virgin Mary or a saint. (When I talk about images, I am referring to a picture, painting, or sculpture.)

It is important that the kids like or relate to the chosen image and that the image be suitable for catechesis. Therefore these images should be natural, appropriate, realistic, simple, and have expressions (sober, joyful, calm) that are not too extreme. Use a picture of the risen Jesus rather than of Jesus crucified. The image of the Good Shepherd also helps.

The images should be of a single color, and we should avoid any accessory elements that could distract or scare children, such as images of the Child Jesus with an open chest or the Sacred Heart of Jesus full of swords; images with blood and thorns; representations of the Virgin surrounded by angels or dominating demons, and so forth.

Be clear that the images are man-made representations and that God is greater than all of them. We should even explain to children how images are made and that nothing happens if an image is broken, aside from the material loss.

The catechist or parent should also explain that Christians do not worship images. Representations of God are only meant to bring us closer to the Lord.

*Elements*

The elements that make up the "Jesus corner" should be carefully selected. We should always aim for appropriateness, good taste, and the constant renewal of any perishable elements such as flowers and the like. The prayer corner should have the following items:

- A small table or shelf with a white tablecloth, which is at a normal height when children are seated
- A Bible
- An image of Jesus
- A vase; the children take turns bringing in flowers
- A small candle
- A rug and some cushions

Make sure the prayer corner does not get cluttered with too many things. It should not become a place where the kids bring all their holy cards, flowers, medals, and so forth. To be effective it must be restrained, with a few core elements that are refreshed from time to time.

## *Its use*

At the beginning of the year, the catechist will pray with the children simply by gathering them in the same place they have their catechesis. After the children have been introduced to silence and prayer, it would be a good idea to set up the prayer corner.

Allow the children to help choose and put together the elements of the prayer corner. The parents should participate in its opening celebration. The prayer corner will be valuable insofar as it is used. If catechists, teachers, and parents are not convinced of its usefulness and do not use it to pray, children will use it even less.

The Bible from the prayer corner is used to read the Word of God in the catechetical meetings. We also use it for daily prayer. The children can go to pray in the Jesus corner either upon arriving or leaving; they can pray before, during, or after recess without asking permission and during activities, but with permission.

When children are in the prayer corner, we do not have to monitor their prayers. If they want to kneel, make gestures, kiss the Bible, sing, or just say a prayer, they need to feel free to express themselves and pray as the Spirit prompts them. What matters most is that they become familiar with the things of God.

A box or small urn in which children can freely deposit their personal intentions can be added to the prayer corner. From time to time, every month, for example, you will need to find the best way to remove the old intentions. They can be put in an envelope and offered at the feet of an image in the church or just burned as a sign they will be going up to God.

Of course, having a corner in which to pray does not necessarily indicate that children will pray more. Prayer is a gift from God and must be transformed into a way of life. A Jesus corner may be one element to help us in this long and beautiful journey of introducing children to prayer.

*The church, the house of God, is the proper place for the liturgical prayer of the parish community. It is also the privileged place for adoration of the real presence of Christ in the Blessed Sacrament. The choice of a favorable place is not a matter of indifference for true prayer.*

*—For personal prayer, this can be a "prayer corner" with the Sacred Scriptures and icons, in order to be there, in secret, before our Father. In a Christian family, this kind of little oratory fosters prayer in common.*

*Catechism of the Catholic Church,* 2691

## Chapter 7
# Prayer in the Family

*Nothing is equal to prayer: it makes the impossible possible and the difficult easy.*
(*Translated from the Spanish*) Attributed to Saint John Chrysostom

Many of the guidelines I have given so far on introducing children to prayer can be used especially by catechists, teachers, and parents of school-age children (starting at age three or four). I consider it important to add some thoughts that may be useful in teaching little ones how to pray, especially within the family.

Regarding teaching prayer to children, parents and other close relatives play a key role. I would even say that without their participation, any attempt to start a child on the path of faith will be rough going, especially in the first years of life.

Parents have a role and a protagonism that cannot be delegated to others, since for many of the children, parents are a reflection of God. Many parents feel that their children are a special gift entrusted to them by God.

As Rose-Marie de Casablanca says, "God, in his infinite love for every being, wants the child to enter into communication with him as soon as he [or she] can. Having created the child 'in his image and likeness,' he has given him that ability, and to help form those bonds of love between the child and him, he gives parents the role of mediators. He also enables them to take on that task to the extent that they pursue their own filial relationship with him."

Children's prayer is built more on a personal relationship with God than on formulas or recited prayers. They learn this relationship from childhood by sensing and touching their parents' attitude.

At first, parents will only be able to pray *for* their children. Shortly after birth, they will have opportunities to gradually introduce their children to the way of prayer, until the children are ready to share prayer with adults and pray on their own.

Following Rose-Marie Casablanca, I will offer some guidelines so that parents and family members can start praying together with their children.

## From conception to the baby's arrival home

Many couples, in their desire to have children, pray for their child even before they conceive.

Pregnancy can be a wonderful opportunity to pray for the unborn child and also for unwanted pregnancies. This authentic prayer associates the unborn child to that same petition. Many parents have the beautiful custom of placing their hands on the mother's belly and raising their prayers together. It's a beautiful and exciting feeling to know one is expecting a child from God.

Gestation, pregnancy, and childbirth are unique experiences that can bring a mother into intense contact with God (if only to offer him the pain of childbirth for her child or for someone else who needs prayer).

Also, the couple's prayer for their child has an impact on their relationship with God and on their own prayer. The arrival of children is a source of blessing and joy for all family members.

Every child, no matter the circumstances of his or her birth, is a gift from God and a reason to pray, especially in difficult situations. For example, parents may pray for the strength to accept and cope with whatever they have to face. In that sense, the silent, helpful, prayerful, ever-attentive presence of the Virgin Mary can be a source of comfort and strength.

## Before the child can walk

Prior to the birth, parents and other family members prayed for the child. After the birth, they will be able to further develop their prayer in front of the baby. Parents "lend" their words, hands, and entire body to the baby to express the prayer that the Holy Spirit inspires in them on the child's behalf.

When parents pray with and for their children, they pray in their name. This is apart from the close conscious-unconscious relationship between mother and child. The example of the parents' contact with God acts on the child, guiding him or her silently to the Lord. Silent prayer is a source of grace for the little one.

Moreover, some tools can foster prayer at these young ages. Parents can complement their prayer by looking for anything that can help children grow into a more prayerful life. Two senses are particularly rich in this regard: seeing and hearing.

Since the baby is able to fix her gaze on her beloved at two weeks of age and can make out quite a bit of what she sees around her at two or three months of age, parents can help her set her gaze on certain objects that enrich her memory in a spiritual sense by placing a religious object next to the crib, preferably next to the baby rather than above her. The religious objects should be suited to a child's mentality; they should be simple and beautiful to the child's eyes.

A second element that tends to impact a child's eyes is light. It would be a good idea to light up the main object at the time of prayer. As for hearing, the baby can internalize both the murmur of her parents' prayer and some simple religious songs they sing to her.

The child's prayer begins in his first months of life, *in utero*. He can be helped along to enter into a relationship with God. In this regard, we distinguish two forms: prayer throughout the day (occasional) and family prayer (more organized).

## *Prayer throughout the day.*

Adults can find many opportunities to help children participate in their own moments of closeness to God. Whether it be a prayer of praise, petition, or thanksgiving, the child participates as if by osmosis, absorbing her parents' attitudes and dispositions. The little one's reactions are usually an endless source of joy and thanksgiving for adults.

## *Family prayer*

Quite a few parents set time aside for family prayer at some point during the day and include the little ones in it. This atmosphere of prayer, the prevailing mood of reaching out to God, penetrates the child's heart in a deep and unfathomable way. When the little one is able to sit up on his own, he can sit on the lap of one of the family members. He may perceive certain gestures of prayer that he can easily grasp, and the child's gestures may also help the parents commit more to prayer.

Far from being artificial and oppressive, family prayer, in its simplicity and with the child's brief and spontaneous participation, is in keeping with a child's actual ability.

Accompanying the development of language, it is good for the child to get used to repeating some words with a religious connotation (such as Jesus; Mary; Thank you, Jesus! I love you, Jesus! Hallelujah! and so forth), gradually discovering their meaning after repeating them over and over again.

# After the child can walk

During this last period that we analyzed, the child's ability to pray has been growing, along with the development of language and an increasing awareness of the child's own personality. Adults play an even more important role insofar as the child is increasingly capable of relating to God.

## *The role of adults.*

Adults are much more able than they think to reestablish a life of relationship with God based on their experiences with their own children. Although many do not know how to pray or what words to say, we learn, as we said before, to pray by praying. Be confident that the Spirit will tell you what to say or do! Prayer is always a source of blessing for everyone.

The parents' task consists essentially in living their faith in the most simple and logical way possible, imbuing their children with a love of God and the need to talk with him. Therefore, it is important for children to participate in their parents' prayer. All other adults around the child (grandparents, aunts and uncles, godparents) can also play a much deeper role to the extent that they enter into a loving relationship with the Lord.

## *Basis of the child's prayerful activity*

Up to three years of age, the child's individual and family prayer life is rapidly evolving, based on his psychomotor development.

## *Prayer with the body*

The child experiences a vital need to move, to use her whole body in everything she does. Thus, gestures, rhythm, dancing, and singing must form the ideal basis for prayer, first by mimicking adults, and then in an ever more spontaneous, even solitary way. Clapping, raising hands, and offering open palms are gestures that leave their mark on a child, as well as the Sign of the Cross.

### *Mental development*

The explosion of language we see in a child who has just learned to walk, the joy he finds in being able to use so many new words, is a special opportunity to help him pray. When a child is able to make himself understood with words, his prayer begins to make more sense.

But the essential thing is always the child's inner attitude rather than the number of prayers she can memorize. Curiosity, the spirit of observation, and the association of ideas are favorable elements for the spiritual life. Everything that is cause for wonder in a child can be a reason for praise and thanksgiving to God for all he has given us.

Language development and the child's keen curiosity give him the urge to ask about everything. This is the age of the "why" questions. We should always give the children realistic and appropriate answers.

## Different occasions to pray

### *Throughout the day.*

Taking into account the different elements we have mentioned, we see that there can be many forms of prayer throughout the day. The important thing is not to talk about God all the time but to live in his presence.

Prayer, then, becomes praise to the Lord, an expression of thanksgiving for the small details of everyday life. In the course of the day, we can thank God for the wonder of the world around us.

This thanksgiving may be accompanied by appropriate songs that children and adults can sing together.

Children express themselves in different ways. Sometimes it will be through a series of brief and joyous invocations (started by the adult and then picked up by the child). There are plenty of big and little topics we can talk to God and Jesus about. Also, all the signs and gestures that accompany the words will help us express the faith experience all over again. In this way, each day can offer a rich array of occasions for prayer.

## *The "family liturgy"*

The child shows a desire to participate actively in prayer that brings the family together. She will want to join in and imitate her family members. The child only understands the general meaning of that gathering, but she intuitively perceives its value (thus, she should not be excluded).

Regardless of whether family prayer is organized or improvised, what the child likes is that her parents pray with her and do not force her to pray. She likes that it is a shared activity without teachers or "supervisors." Of course, it will have to be adapted to the needs of young children. Once again, the more involved the body and the senses are in prayer, the more it will engage the child.

At the same time, we must take into account the child's character, personal rhythm, individual characteristics, and personality. The young one's participation in family prayer should be brief, joyful, and heartfelt. If family prayer continues on, the child may freely go. The bottom line is that the child should feel free; parents should respect her desire or rejection. In this way, her participation in prayer will only bring benefits. God is to be discovered in freedom and in love, not in morality, obligation, and guilt.

*Liturgical ceremonies.*

Soon the child will have the opportunity to attend and participate in liturgical ceremonies like the Mass or other major religious celebrations.

In the Mass, we should hold to the same principle as in a family gathering of some importance. Young children are usually present, participating insofar as they can, doing other activities or just playing. What we must ensure is that the presence of children in the Mass does not disturb the celebration. Children should feel comfortable in the house of God, so it may help to let them take along some of their toys, books, or drawing materials.

As this attitude may annoy some people, it is preferable to attend children's Masses, where everyone knows the celebration will be more "lively" and active due to the presence of children. These Masses are conceived and organized for little ones, but they can often be a source of blessings for adults.

Major religious holidays should become a special opportunity for children to grasp their religious meaning and have a particular encounter with God. On such feast days (Christmas, Easter, Pentecost, saint's feast day) children must be taken into account so that they feel actively involved.

Thus, we conclude that the family is a privileged place of encounter between children and God. Parents are first and foremost servants and mediators between God and the little ones he has entrusted to them. God works through them, with them, and in them. The important thing is to let yourself be led by God so that this stage leads the children to awaken to the spirit of prayer, to a direct relationship with "their" God.

*God loves our families, despite so many wounds and divisions. The presence of Christ invoked through family prayer helps us overcome problems, heal wounds, and open up paths of hope. Many inadequacies in the home can be offset by services provided by the ecclesial community, family of families.... The example of prayer of their parents and grandparents is important for [children's] whole life; it is their mission to teach their children and grandchildren their first prayers.*

Final Aparecida document, 119 and 441

*At the heart of catechesis we find, in essence, a Person, the Person of Jesus of Nazareth, "the only Son from the Father... full of grace and truth," who suffered and died for us and who now, after rising, is living with us forever. It is Jesus who is "the way, and the truth, and the life....Accordingly, the definitive aim of catechesis is to put people not only in touch but in communion, in intimacy, with Jesus Christ: only He can lead us to the love of the Father in the Spirit and make us share in the life of the Holy Trinity.*

*Catechesi Tradendae*, 5

# Conclusion

*For me, prayer is a surge of the heart; it is a simple look turned toward heaven, it is a cry of recognition and of love, embracing both trial and joy.*

(*Translated from the Spanish*)
Attributed to Saint Therese of the Child Jesus

Whenever I write about these topics, I am left with two sensations that are sometimes opposed. One is the sense that there is still so much to reflect on and research that these pages are just a start. The other is that when it comes to God and the faith, what matters most is God's action, his grace, and then all of our reflections are just that: mere human reflections.

Nevertheless, I think the attempt to share and systematize these experiences enriches us and helps us grow in the faith. Only what we live and reflect on as a community can allow us to draw ever closer to the endless mystery of God. God wants whatever we say about him to be shared with others in the community, in the people of God, in the Church.

In these reflections, I have tried to make a small contribution to the efforts of catechists and parents at introducing children to silence and prayer. Obviously, it is not a simple topic, and we have to keep going back over our work to see if we are really helping the kids pray more and better.

As I said at the beginning, we learn to pray by praying. But it is also true that if we stop for a bit, we can gather experiences about children's prayer. Sometimes it is a matter of sitting down to observe, to see what the children do and need regarding prayer, and to keep motivating them to continue in that direction.

Almost without realizing it, we end up becoming "teachers of prayer" for our children. It is not a matter of working out big theories or writing treatises on children's prayer; fundamentally, it is a matter of our praying first so that they can follow us.

And of course, prayer is always a gift from God. And like any gift, it is not something we can merit; we do not achieve it by our own effort or sacrifice. God gives the gift of prayer to each one however he wishes, for it is the Lord we should ask to teach us to pray. Jesus himself promised us the help of the Holy Spirit, who will enlighten our hearts so that we can call God "Abba," which means "Daddy."

Luis M. Benavides

If you have any suggestions, comments, or questions about any of my courses, you can e-mail me at **lmbenavides@arnet.com.ar** or **lmbenavides@gmail.com.ar**, or visit my web page at **www.luis-benavides.go.to.**

# Bibliography

Aldazábal, José. *Gestos y símbolos* ("Gestures and Symbols"). Dossiers CPL 40. Barcelona: Centro de Pastoral Litúrgica de Barcelona, 1990.

Alexandre, Dolores y Berrueta, Teresa. *Iniciar en la oración* ("Introduction to Prayer"). Madrid: Editorial CCS, 1995.

Benavides, Luis M. *Cuentos para ser humano* ("Tales About Humanity"). Buenos Aires: Editorial SB, 2007.

Benavides, Luis y Pandolfi, María Emilia. *El Rosario contado a los niños* ("Explaining the Rosary to Children"). Edit. Bonum. Bs.As., 2003.

Benavides, Luis M. *La catequesis con niños pequeños* ("Catechesis for Young Children"). Buenos Aires: Editorial SB, 2010.

Benavides, Luis M. *Metodología catequística para niños* ("Methodology for Catechetizing Children"). Ediciones PPC/SM: Madrid, 2005; Buenos Aires, 2007.

Benavides, Luis M. *Temas difíciles con niños* ("Explaining Difficult Topics to Children"). Buenos Aires: Ed. PPC, 2012.

Benavides, Luis M. *¡S.O.S., catequesis! Hacia nuevos rumbos en la catequesis* ("S.O.S., Catechesis! Towards New Places in Catechesis"). Buenos Aires: Editorial SB, 2009; Argentina: Mención de Honor Feria del Libro Católico de Argentina, 2010.

Caballero, Nicolás. *Dentro, tú eres silencio* ("Silence Within You"). Buenos Aires: Editorial Claretiana, 1999.

Cánepa, Marta. *¿Cómo hablar de Dios a los más pequeños?* ("How to Talk to Young Children About God"). Buenos Aires: Edic. Paulinas, 1994.

Casiello, Beatriz. *Metodología catequística* ("Methodology for Catechesis"). Buenos Aires: Guadalupe, 1986.

*Catecismo de la Iglesia Católica* (*Catechism of the Catholic Church*). Buenos Aires: Oficina del Libro. Conferencia Episcopal Argentina, 2003.

Catequistas del IPA. *Metodología catequística, cuaderno 1* ("Methodology for Catechesis," Book 1) y *Camina en mi presencia* Cuad. Nº 2 ("Walk in My Presence," Book 2). Buenos Aires: Ed. Stella, 1985.

Cavalca, Flavio y Montanhese Ivo. *La oración del niño* ("Children's Prayer"). Bogotá: Edic. San Pablo, 1994.

Conferencia Episcopal Argentina. *Bases para la catequesis de iniciación* ("Basis for the First Catechesis"). Buenos Aires: Edic. Don Bosco, 1981.

Conferencia Episcopal Latinoamericana (CELAM). *Documento Final de Aparecida* (Final Document of Aparecida). Buenos Aires: Ed. Paulinas, 2007.

Del Bueno de Morrone, Lidia. *Creciendo con Dios* ("Growing Up With God"). Buenos Aires: Ed. Bonum, 1992.

Dotro, Ricardo y García Helder, Gerardo. *Diccionario de Liturgia* ("Dictionary of Liturgy"). Buenos Aires: Ediciones AMICO, 2002.

Equipo. *Celebrar Misa con Niños* ("Celebrating Mass with Children"). Buenos Aires: Ed. Paulinas/Marova, 1981.

Equipo de catequesis. *Nuestro Padre Dios* ("God Our Father"). Buenos Aires: Edic. Búsqueda, 1974.

García Ahumada, Enrique. *Comunicación audiovisual para evangelizar* ("Evangelizing in Audiovisual Communication"). Santiago de Chile: Editorial Tiberíades, 1999.

García, Eduardo. *Gloria a ti, Señor, porque nos amas: Sugerencias para la celebración de la Eucaristía con niños* ("Glory Be to You, Lord, Because You Love Us: Suggestions for the Mass With Children"). Buenos Aires: Ediciones Paulinas, 1996.

Guardini, Romano. *Los signos sagrados* ("Sacred Signs"). Buenos Aires: Edic. Librería Emanuel, 1983.

Godin, André. *Adulto y niño ante Dios* ("Adults and Children Before God"). Salamanca: Edic. Sígueme, 1968.

Henderson, Feliciy. *Mis libritos de oraciones* ("My Prayer Booklets"). Buenos Aires: Editorial Lumen, 1995.

Jálics, Francisco. *Aprendiendo a orar* ("Learning to Pray"). Buenos Aires: Ed. Paulinas, 1984.

Larrañaga, Ignacio. *El silencio de María* ("The Silence of Mary"). Buenos Aires: Ed. Paulinas, 1975.

Lefebvre, X. y Perin, L. *El niño ante Dios* ("The Child Before God"). Bilbao: Ed. Desclee de Brower, 1981.

Lubienska de Lenval. *La liturgia del gesto* ("The Liturgy of Gesture"). San Sebastián: Ed. DINOR, 1957.

Miani, Marcelino. *Los signos sacramentales* ("Sacramental Signs"). Buenos Aires: Ed. Claretiana, 1980.

Pomme D'Api. *El despertar religioso de los niños* ("Spiritual Awakening for Children"). Barcelona: Ed. Claretiana, 1981.

Rose-Marie de Casablanca. *El niño capaz de Dios* ("Child's Capacity for God"). Bilbao: Edic. Mensajero, 1991.

Scarpazza, Benigno. *Ayudemos a los hijos a encontrar a Dios* ("Helping Our Children Find God"). Bogotá: Ed. Paulinas, 1991.

Sagrada Congregación para el Clero. *Directorio general para la catequesis* ("General Directory for Catechesis"). Buenos Aires: Oficina del Libro. Conferencia Episcopal Argentina, 1997.

Tschirch, Reinmar. *Dios para niños* ("God for Children"). Santander: Ed. Sal Terrae, 1981.

Vila-Boas, Magda. *Ejercicios de relajación para niños* ("Relaxation Exercises for Children"). Buenos Aires: Edic. Paulinas, 1995.

# Other Liguori Publications Titles for Children and Families...

## Sharing the Faith With Your Child
*From Birth to Age Four*

ISBN: 978-0-7648-1523-2

With practical wisdom, the authors of this handbook show parents how their daily lives, experiences, and relationships reinforce their role as parents. The book includes chapters on Parenting, Being a Family, Being a Catholic Family, and Rearing Children in a Christian Family.

## Handbook for Today's Catholic Children

ISBN: 978-0-7648-1013-8

Written for younger children, *Handbook for Today's Catholic Children* presents basic tenets of the Catholic faith in terms they can understand. Chapter topics include "All About Sin—More About Love," and "The Church Cares for You," which discusses the Ten Commandments. Each chapter ends with a short prayer.

### To Order Visit Your Local Bookstore
### Call 800-325-9521 • Visit liguori.org

Liguori Publications offers many titles as eBooks through leading distributors such as Amazon, Barnes & Noble, Kobo, and iTunes

# Other Liguori Publications Titles for Children and Families...

These two new books, by Father Joe Kempf and his furry friend, Big Al, are written the way children talk—and the way they think! Read the prayers and listen to the CDs with a child you love as Father Joe and Big Al introduce these prayers read by children.

## My Sister Is Annoying!
*And Other Prayers for Children*

ISBN: 978-0-7648-1827-1

*My Sister is Annoying* is a beautifully illustrated, fun way for children to talk to God about things that are important to them.

## You Want Me To Be Good ALL DAY?
*And Other Prayers for Children*

ISBN: 978-0-7648-1843-1

In a delightful combination of events that impact children's lives, Big Al learns lessons including compassion, responsibility, and individuality through prayer. Prayers about Baptism, Communion, and even a wedding make this book perfect for young children.

### To Order Visit Your Local Bookstore
### Call 800-325-9521 • Visit liguori.org

Liguori Publications offers many titles as eBooks through leading distributors such as Amazon, Barnes & Noble, Kobo, and iTunes